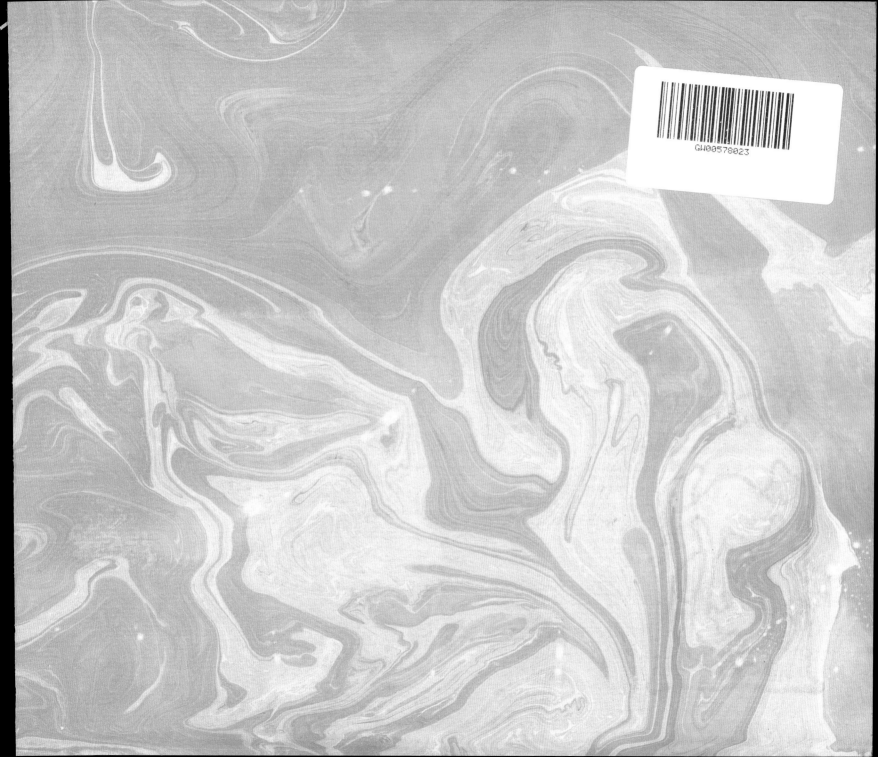

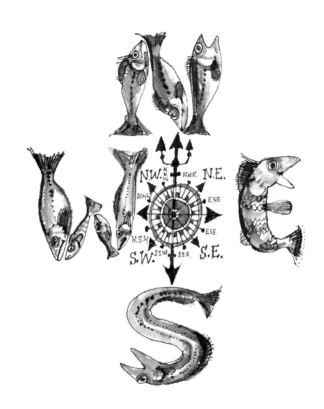

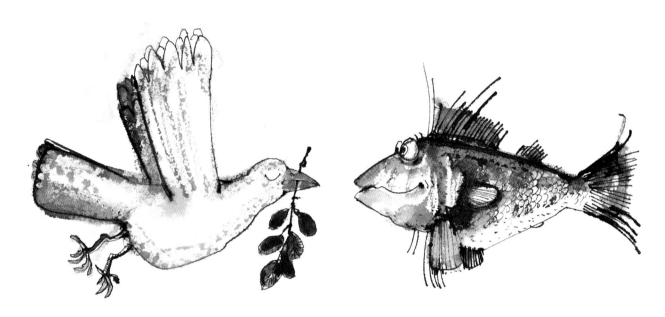

OCTOPOLIS TO HALKI

OCTOPOLIS

Graham Clarke's

OCTOPOLIS TO HALKI

EBENEZER PRESS

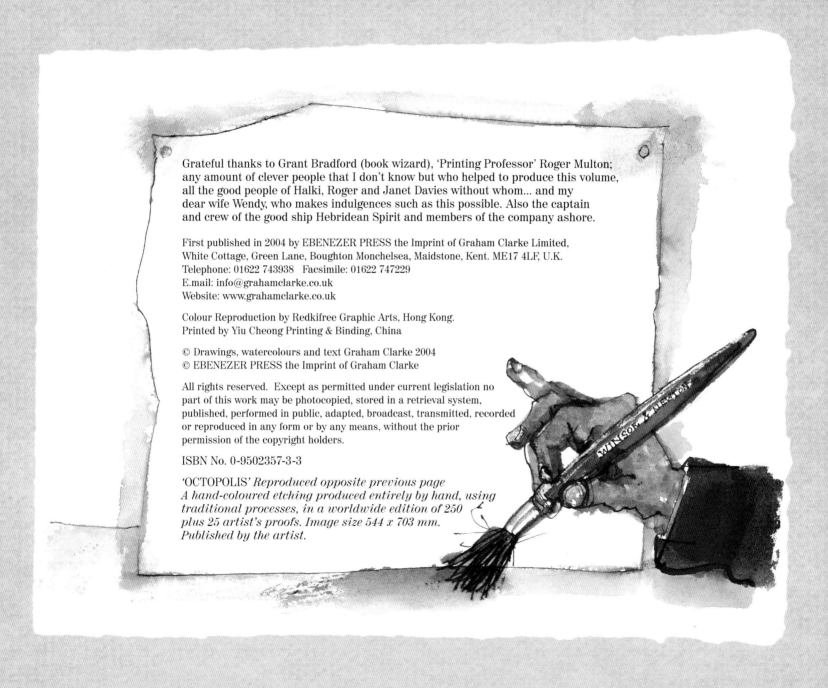

Grateful thanks to Grant Bradford (book wizard), 'Printing Professor' Roger Multon; any amount of clever people that I don't know but who helped to produce this volume, all the good people of Halki, Roger and Janet Davies without whom... and my dear wife Wendy, who makes indulgences such as this possible. Also the captain and crew of the good ship Hebridean Spirit and members of the company ashore.

First published in 2004 by EBENEZER PRESS the Imprint of Graham Clarke Limited, White Cottage, Green Lane, Boughton Monchelsea, Maidstone, Kent. ME17 4LF, U.K.
Telephone: 01622 743938   Facsimile: 01622 747229
E.mail: info@grahamclarke.co.uk
Website: www.grahamclarke.co.uk

Colour Reproduction by Redkifree Graphic Arts, Hong Kong.
Printed by Yiu Cheong Printing & Binding, China

ISBN No. 0-9502357-3-3

'OCTOPOLIS' *Reproduced opposite previous page*
A hand-coloured etching produced entirely by hand, using traditional processes, in a worldwide edition of 250 plus 25 artist's proofs. Image size 544 x 703 mm. Published by the artist.

YES this is a book of pictures but all this lettering took him a long long time to do...

It must have done

It did.

So he would.........

all by hand?

all by hand.

So he would be very much obliged if you could bother to read some of it.

Even if you didn't pay for it and it was a present?

Yes, 'fraid so....

oooh.

Look.. I may be only a mollusk but let me tell you this is an exellent book.

MMM..

WISE WINKLE

ADVERTISMENT
That limpet on the bottom left hand corner of this page knows what he's talking about. This is the best book what that I've ever read.

Winkles can't read

and you can't talk you're a fish...

You see?

He's left an 'E' out of ADVERTISMENT Wendy says.

" of Greek islands in general and Halki in particular. "

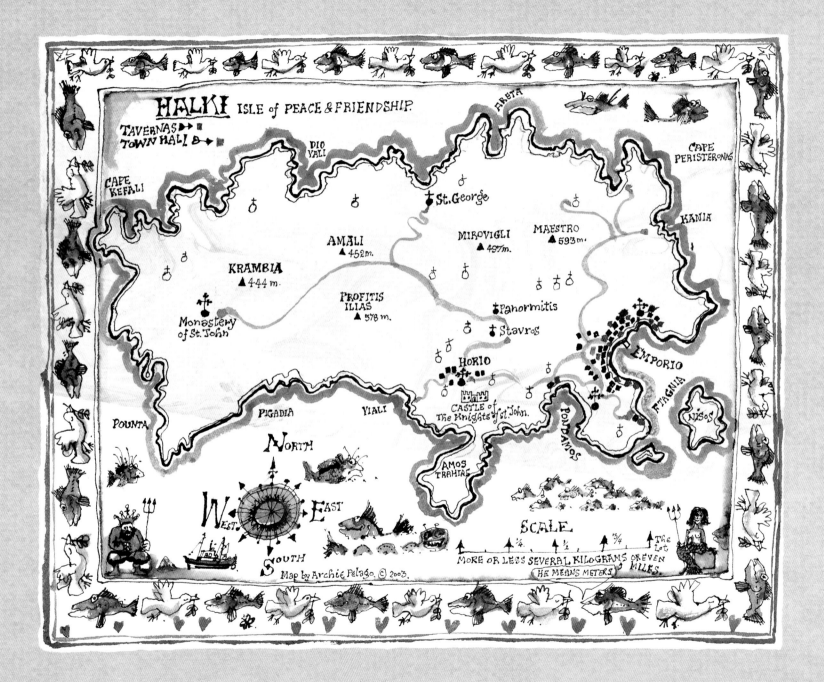

HALKI ISLE of PEACE & FRIENDSHIP

TAVERNAS ►►
TOWN HALL ►►►

FRETA

CAPE PERISTERONAS

DIO VALI

CAPE KEFALI

St. George

KANIA

MIROVIGLI
△ 497m.

MAESTRO
△ 593 m.

AMALI
△ 452 m.

KRAMBIA
△ 444 m.

PROFITIS ILIAS
△ 578 m.

Monastery of St. John

Panormitis

Stavros

EMPORIO

HORIO

POUNTA

PIGADIA

YIALI

CASTLE of The Knights of St. John

FTAGNIA

PONDAMOS

NISOS

AMOS TRAHIAS

North

West · East

South

SCALE

MORE OR LESS SEVERAL KILOGRAMS OR EVEN MILES
(HE MEANS METERS)
¼   ½   ¾   The Lot

Map by Archie Pelago. © 2003.

OCTOPOLIS

In April 2002 my Wendy and I realised a long held dream and joined a beautiful little ship to sail the Greek Islands. She was the Hebridean Spirit and is something of a legend in the travel business being quite unlike the much larger vessels that ply the same trade. Small enough indeed to pass through the Corinth Canal and enter harbours and anchorages forbidden to larger craft.

All too soon our time aboard came to an end having fulfilled the dream beyond dreaming. With much reluctance we said our goodbyes to the lovely crew and after a noisy lunch in Rhodes with our fellow passengers we flew back to reality.

All the beautiful islands worked their magic and in due course I completed one of my larger etchings. "Octopolis."

⟵ AGHIOS PANTELEMON, RHODES

Amongst our circle of very good friends are Roger & Janet, on one of their regular visits to my studio they spotted octopolis and shouted Halki! very loudly too in Rogers case.

mmm...

For some time they and other grateful English visitors had wanted to present a gift to the island in memory of dear Halki friends now passed away and in gratitude for many wonderful holidays. Octopolis it was decided 'filled the bill'.

Accordingly a framed octopolis was transported, followed a week or two later by Roger, Janet, Wendy and I. It was thought that the council chamber of the fine Town Hall should be its home together with a framed message of dedication.

At a very jolly ceremony on a lovely Saturday evening in May 2003 Octopolis was duly handed over to the newly appointed mayor. Speeches, shouting, laughter and crisps marked the occasion, history and lasting friendships were made.

Page 11

YOUR OCTOPUS

Surely your octopus is one of the strangest of all GOD's creatures. So powerful and dangerous when alive so we are informed by the few brave survivors of underwater encounters but so marvellously floppy and loose limbed when deceased. Comes from not owning a decent skellington of course.

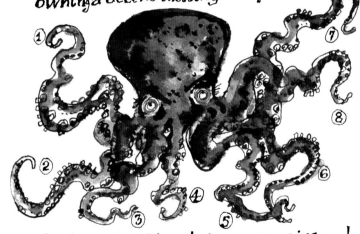

We learn that they do have memories and are by far the most intelligent of the mollusc family.

"NOT THAT THERE'S MUCH COMPETITION."

"WATCH IT MATEY."

It was Friday afternoon a very very long time ago. God had been busy creating molluscs all week and was tired. He was pleased with his work though, scallops, whelks, winkles, cockies and mussels all in beautiful shells and oysters too which were to prove such a delight to mankind when He eventually found time to finalise His work in the monkey department.

As we know molluscs in general don't have many legs so amongst the so far unused items was a big pile of them also a floppy sort of head which for some reason sported a beak and two large beady eyes. But there were no proper bodies and all the shells had been used up before lunch.

SORRY ABOUT THE SPLODGE

But He thought, it would be such a shame to let these bits go to waste.....

[ENCYCLOPAEDIA ANACHRONOLOGICA Vol XXXI ch. 185]

Paros Greengrocer

He bides his time while the elderly customer evaluates a melon. Neither are in any great hurry it seems to complete any transaction. The little chapel of Ai-Nikolas on the quayside at Paroikia provides a little shade for him to set up shop and a convenient shelf for his refreshments.

Kg.

SOLD

Page No.15

FISH PIAGGIO

Not much more than a box and a motor scooter, how we love these little vehichles, especially this one so tastefully decorated by the fishmonger himself. I found this example on the island of Patmos, or maybe it was Paros or Poros, probably not Paxos and definately not Pigtrots or Pyrex.

Anyway it was parked (or moored) close by the fishing boats on the quayside so we can assume that the produce must be perfectly fresh, the customer though has apparently some doubts and is taking her time making up her mind.

This is Page 16.

✱ Note the eyelashes on the headlamps.

MMM....

" ....Then after Christmas, the childrens presents safely delivered they put their nice black hats back on and go back to their ordinary job. "

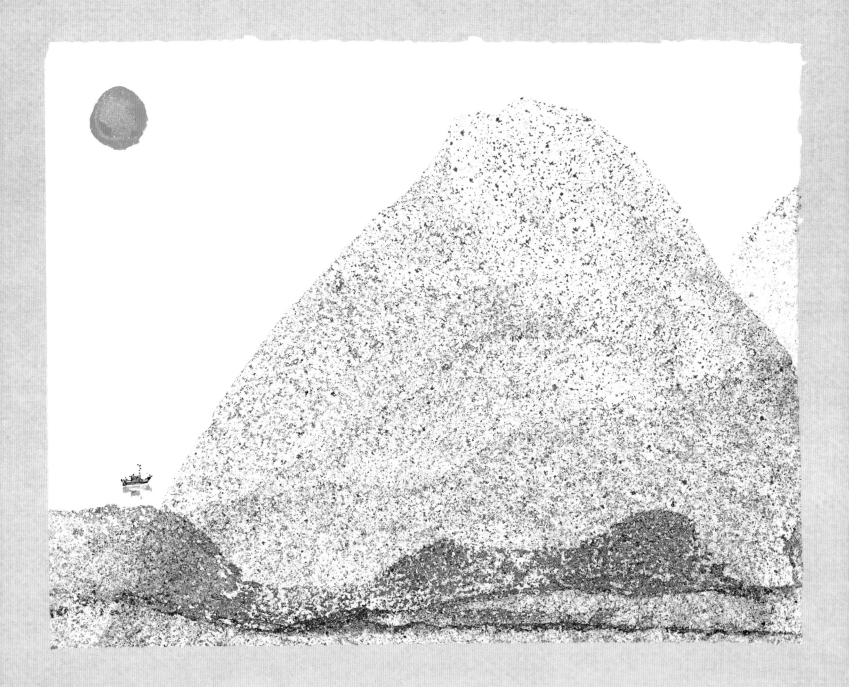

"CREATE YOUR OWN GREEEK ISLAND"

Simply cut out all the elements provided, position the windmills near the top and the taverna near the bottom then scatter your chapels at random avoiding the sea and sky, paste down carefully.

Proffessionals tip. For added realism and that authentic aroma of the quayside stick your cutouts using fishpaste.

We are reliably informed that St. John the Divine wrote the Book of Revelation on Patmos sitting in a cave up the hill. Though quite old this man of God quietly conducting his studies while sitting on the chapel yard wall enjoying a nice cup of coffee, probably is not him.

ARTISTS NOTE
I don't know where this place is, but it would take more than a couple of ouzos to get me up there.

and 24.

SOHLAW *

The fisherman attends to his nets and lines, carefully observed by several interested parties hoping to experience his customary generosity. But what is that shoe doing I hear you ask, surely not to chuck at the cats?

Perish the thought, his bare right foot, particularly the bit between the big toe and the next make a third hand, very useful for such intricate stringy work, and the unravelling of knotty and netty problems.

It's true.

So where are you rushing off to?

The O'Limpet Games of course.

*

For those readers not acquainted with a certain brand of Greek beer, our man is sitting on an upturned crate that once contained the very stuff.

You will probably have noticed as I certainly have that fishmongers are almost invariably very jolly folk, it's a wonderful thing and adds to the already joyful activity of the purchasing of fish. Given the lugubrious visage of most of the articles lying on the slab, it is probably natures way of compensating for their sad and dismal appearance.

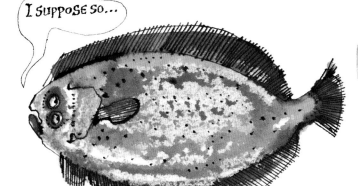

I suppose so...

 poor old sole  mmm...

ARTISTS NOTE

Experience and diligent research reveal that an artist hoping to paint difficult bottle labels will find it less difficult if he refrains from opening it until the job is done.

ALL ABOARD

(ON PAGE No. 29)

Two nice little fat ferry boats take turns to get you to and from Halki. They depart from Kamiros Skala halfway down the west coast of Rhodes, it's hardly a port, not much more than a quay with a few lovely fishing boats, a bus stop and a couple of tavernas.

Roger & Janet were greeted warmly by swarthy captain and crew and we were off.
The bar was open, the sea was calm and there was a welcome cooling breeze. Suddenly, from down below two fearsome men leaped upon us, far more piratical than our skipper, shouting loudly they grabbed Roger and obviosly wanted to chuck him overboard.

Would they make off with our womenfolk too? No, it was Yiannis and Nikolias father and son fishermen from Halki, old friends of R&J and in fact to be our hosts on the island. Greetings were yelled, introductions made, the ladies embraced and cheerful toothless grins reasured us.

The island comes into view soon after we set sail a grey misty mountain floating on the silver sea. Past small islets, one apparently bearing nothing but a solitary goat. Then past Alimnia now deserted.

Emporio, Halkis harbour town of white houses reveals itself like dice scattered from a bucket, then we can make out the famous clock tower and villa Sophia where we are to stay. This is going to be good.

Isle of Peace and Friendship

In 1983 UNESCO together with the Greek Government designated Halki an island of Peace and Friendship and quite right too. As part of the deal many of the fine Italianate ruined houses were to be restored. There is little evidence of UNESCO now but little Halki is without doubt peaceful and friendly.

During our short stay I feel confident that we made a contribution towards friendship, with regard to 'peace' however (in the sense of quietude) I am not so sure, my Wendy has a famously startling laugh of great carrying power and my squeeze box is quite loud and surprisingly penetrating for one so small so they tell me.

These factors combined with the very jolly disposition of our fellow visitors and dear hosts might well have busted the islands decibel counter, which it does not have.

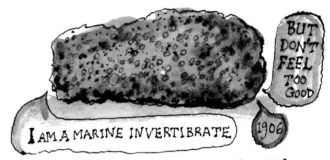

I AM A MARINE INVERTIBRATE

BUT DON'T FEEL TOO GOOD

1906

The devastating sponge blight of the early 1900s caused mass emigration reducing the population from 3000 to 300, many went to Florida U.S of A. Very useful monies are sent 'home' for good works hence the one and only road bearing the unlikely name of **TARPON SPRINGS BOULEVARD.**

PEACE & FRIENDSHIP

So was it the sponges or the people that went to America?

I'll give you three guesses......

30

O2H & H2O

'Octopolis to Halki' in the language of electronical communicals and digital fidgets known as 'texting' can be rendered p simly as O2H.

"So What?" I hear you ask. Well nothing really, I just wanted to mention it, this is my book after all.

However, when it comes to the subject of H2O it is of much greater interest and of vital importance especially on Halki.

Once upon a time Halki had all the fresh water it required, so lots of lovely green grass for cows, two crops a year from the fields and a nice bath whenever you fancied it, not just on your birthday.

Anyway, maybe they dug their wells too deep, they turned salty with seawater and others dried up altogether. Beautiful though ~~though~~ (sorry) the island certainly is it might well be described as arid.

Fresh water nowadays comes from Rhodes in the water boat and is indeed a precious commodity. "Waste not," for in the busy season there may be no water for days not even enough to make your ouzo go cloudy, strong men have been known to weep.

Ouzo for a Boozo?

But Raki for the Halkiholic.

EMERY

e 200 ml · 38% VOL.

ΟΥΖΟ

FERT

ΡΟΔΙΝΙ

ΠΑΡΑΓΩΓΗ - ΕΜΦΙΑΛΩΣΗ
EMERY A.E. ΡΟΔΟΣ

5 20 1806. 101037

TOURISTS & VISITORS

You can't be a tourist on Halki.
You can be on Rhodes, mainland
Greece, Europe, North America or
the whole World but on tiny Halki
with only one road and a few bits of
track only a few kilometers length
in total you cannot exactly "tour."

He's quite right.

yes, he occasionally is......

You are able however to take vigourous
walks, gentle toddles or delightful
boat trips. On Halki you're a visitor
and a fortunate and most welcome
one too.

page 34.

TOWN HALL EMPORIO

A very acceptable legacy of the
long Italian occupation and one of
my favourite buildings anywhere,
also home to my etching 'Octopolis'
which hangs in the council chamber.

It's true...

It serves as a meeting place for the
whole community with wonderful views
of the town below with its fine harbour
and out across the blue blue seas to
Alimnia and Rhodes away beyond.
Eleni surveys all this from the bal-
cony outside her mayoral office
window.

Eleni is the mayor

Those Italians certainly didn't make
it easy to draw though, there is a
definate touch of the octopuses about
the front steps.

On the terrace looking across the azure sea towards Rhodes Soufoula takes a well deserved rest from tending her goats, sheep, hens, menfolk and visitors.
Husband Yiannis prepares his long-lines for tomorrows fishing, carefully ordering hundreds of hooks around the rim of a plastic bongo.

Soufoula has removed her Nana Mouskouri glasses for the occasion and her tablecloth turban for sun protection. Yiannis needs no such thing, he has a head of hair that is truly wonderful. A wire wool crash helmet. I believe they are about to offer me another glass of ouzo.

12

OUZO

1880

THE TRADITIONAL GREEK SPIRIT

ΑΔΕΛΦΟΤ Ν. ΚΑΛΟΓΙΑΝΝΗ ΑΕΒΕ

SAINT NIKOLIAS ?

A handsome looking icon chap in the wonderful little church below the castle at Horio on Halki. He bears a remarkable resemblance to our good fisherman friend Nikolias son of our kind hosts.

He looks rather concerned as well as holy, has he made a spelling mistak on his manuscript or is he wondering why his right hand looks so peculiar. He and I both wish it looked better but it didn't so it doesn't.

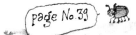

page No. 39

KAPITAN NIKOLIAS

Yiannis & Nikolias aboard their fine boat, the biggest and best equiped on Halki.

Just now they are fishing for GARIDES (shrimp) using the flattish wire mesh pots piled on the stern. They are baited with a dough of oil and flour and set several meters apart at a depth of 60 meters they tell us.

A conversation between father and son sounds like a verbal swordfight, loud stabbing and very fierce, it is not of course it is simply the volume required on board ship with the engine noise and a stiff breeze to cope with.

The fact that they forget to adjust the volume when at home is (as they say in Greece) "Ohi drama".*

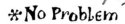

*No Problem

⅔ actual size

41

Piracy on the HIGH SEAS,
the LOW SEAS

AND THE MIDDLE C'S

NEVER MIND. AS LONG HE CONDUCTS HIMSELF PROPERLY....

Raniceps Raninus

Yiannis presents a bag of fish, fifteen fish and I can't give a name to any of them. To my eye they are beautiful, all except No.1 (see opposite ➤➤), later I looked him up in my book. He was a Lesser Forkbeard (Raniceps Raninus) in Germany a Froschquappe and in France Grenouille de Mer. What the Greeks call him I don't know but I bet it isn't ADONIS. But into my Bait Box Stew he went along with olive oil, a tin of anchovies, a couple of lovely oranges, onions, tomatoes, a bottle of retsina, cayenne and black pepper, lots of bay leaves, garlic, Metaxa brandy and ouzo.

It seemed only right to offer our hosts a sample of the finished product and they declared it "Oreya!" which I understand was a very favourable response from Yiannis and Nikolais, then I spotted Souphoula rinsing her mouth out under the kitchen tap.

It should be noted that fishes Nos. 12 – 15 were drawn from 'memory' following some celebratory raki.

page 42.

HALKI HONEY

To be honest (which I occasionally am) I don't know too much about beekeeping; being a devout coward it all looks too dangerous to me.

Halki bees it would appear are especially fortunate, living as they do in these pleasant one two and three storey hives in charming rural surroundings. The honey they make is excellent and the island claims that it is the best in the entire universe.

As you see there are several rocks placed on top of each hive, is this to prevent the little rascals bursting forth through the roof? or to prevent those goats getting in from above? Or simply to make a few less things to trip over when beekeeping at night?

The hives are painted that special blue, the one we see on the roofs and domes of churches and nice little chapels all around us. Do the priests own the hives? Have the beekeepers stolen the paint from the church or do they (or their bees) just like the colour? So many questions, so few answers, such lovely honey.

ΠΑΡΑΓΩΓΟΣ:
ΤΣΟΥΡΟΥΤΤΗΣ ΒΑΣΙΛΗΣ ΜΠΙΝΗΣ
ΤΗΛ 45268 - ΧΑΛΚΗ - ΔΩΔ)ΗΝΣΟΣ

Page 45.

FOWL PLAY

Once or twice a day old Soufoula is to be seen doing her egg hunting. Her flock of hens inhabit an area of the island undefined and unfenced for there are no foxes, and dogs are always secured at night.

She is very wary of sunshine; an abundant commonity on Halki, so she wears a tablecloth on her head in the form of a large loose turban, usually her Nana Moscouri glasses with her dark eyes peering through are the only part of her visage to be seen.

She carries a very stout stick, with which to poke about for eggs amongst all the clutter that would be her front garden if she wasn't married to a fisherman, so it's upturned boats, coils of rope, decaying oil drums, floats, broken oars and shrimp pots.

47.

In the rock strewn field that is her back garden are old packing cases, olive oil tins, beer crates and what might have been in a former life the front counter of a fish and chip shop. Together with rusty kettles, these provide the cosy nesting boxes for her hens on the interior and nice perches for the cockerels on top.

How one loves to hear a cockerel crow in the early morning and in the daytime too if he has good cause. For some reason Soufoula's also let rip in the middle of the night. Why? We do not know, but this is a Greek island.

For such a small population Halki has a remarkable number of tavernas and bars and not a duff one amongst them. During a weeks visit with not too much self catering and lunch and dinner elsewhere you could visit all of them at least once and many more if you take the odd coffee, beer or ouzo. As one does.

All but two are gathered around the harbour, the others being at Pondamos and Ftagnia.

All the tavernas use nice paper table-cloths, most suitable for visiting artists to draw upon and so much app-reciated all round. "Thus many minor masterpieces" were created as the evenings went on and several are now nicely framed and hang on the walls of the homes of fellow inebriants.

MASTERPIECES?

48.

SUNDAY MORNING

Beautiful incantations coming from the direction of the lovely church across the harbour.

There are two distinctly different voices, one no doubt is Halki's very own handsome black gowned priest that we see several times each day along the waterfront, eating breakfast maybe in Dimitri's (the famous bakers) or enjoying a nice cup of coffee in one of the tavernas. The other may be the khaki one that I noticed yesterday, possibly a visiting chaplain for the soldier boys up on the hill.

I should have gone into the church and had I known you can come and go just as you please would have certainly done so, all that is requested is that you buy a candle.

....Sounds fair enough to me.

The churchyard is paved with the extraordinary mosaics called Hokláki intricate figurative and abstract designs made entirely from small black, white and occasionally rusty red pebbles, millions of them A marvellous work of art of great skill and devotion, and like so many such things made by that most modest of artists Anon.

So why didn't he draw us properly?

Too difficult for him I expect...

PAVING BENEATH THE CHURCH TOWER

LITTLE CHAPEL Nº HORIO

✱ ARTIST'S NOTE (ON PAGE 50.)
They really <u>are</u> nice cats on HALKI
It's just that I'm not too good at
drawing them. G.C.

OF HALKI CATS

As we all know cats and fishing villages
invariably go together but in the
majority of such places however beautiful
they be the feline inhabitants are usually
something of a disgrace, eyes, ears
and tails missing bits of fur and good
manners.

Not so on Halki, the cats are clean, bodily
complete and very polite, they do not
climb upon taverna tables and do not
suffer from mange or over population.
They are cared for by kind English ladies
who provide them with real cat food.
Also nice lady vets visit Halki whenever they can to 'see to' the cats in as
pleasant a way as possible.

So why are they so interested in the
activities of the fishermen and look
as though they are hoping for a fishy
snack? I believe it is simply out of
politeness and a sense of tradition,
their duty to take an interest in
quayside activities just as their
scrofulous, one eyed, flea-ridden
old grandfathers did.

52

I have more than a dozen so called guide books to the Greek Islands, only about half of them even give little Halki a mention. Where they do it is variously refered to as Halki, Chalki or even Khalki, and it appears that the writer has probably never even visited the place.

The exceptions to this are good as far as they go but all too brief to do justice.

This book which is by no means a guide book is an attempt to make amends and to say thankyou to all Halki friends and friends of Halki. It is also dedicated to captain and crew of the good ship Hebridean Spirit and my fellow bilge rats thereon.

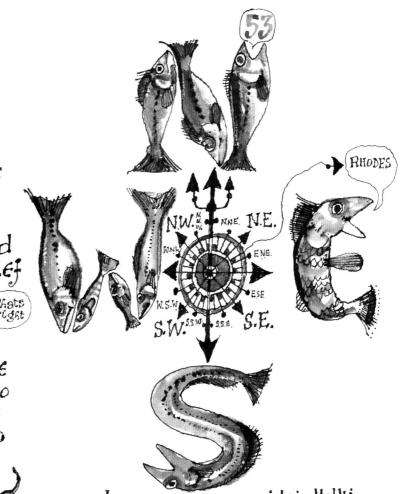

Simply stand on the quayside in Halki facing North. Hold this page in front of you, your HALKI COMPASS is now ready for use.

HORIO

Whether you call it Horio or Chorio, it's a few kilometers from Emporio, it's the old 'capital'. In earlier times Horio was the refuge from pirates, robbers, brigands, buccaneers, plunderers, corsairs, despoilers, bandoleros, desperados, looters, sackers and looters, other kinds of looters (even worse), marauders, vandals, picaroons, various unscrupulos persons, ruffians, and all manner of seaborne unwelcome visitors.

otherwise o.k.?

No, in 1658 a terrible man by the name of Morozinis came all the way from Venice with a huge fleet of ships with the intention of being nasty to Rhodes. They were too much for him so he set about poor little Halki. Most of the inhabitants climbed up to the castle and were safe but others had hidden in a cave on the mountain. Unable to capture the castle even with his great army, he cut down the almond trees, made a big fire and suffocated all the poor people in their hiding place.

✝ ✝ ✝ ✝ ✝

Horio was 'deserted' some years ago but is no longer, several of the ancient houses having been restored and occupied. It is in a wonderful position high up in a cleft in the hills. And above is the famous Castle of the Knights of St. John which incorporates the materials of even older buildings on the same site. A bit of a climb to get up there but well worth it.

spectacular views.

How do you know you're just a fish.

He is right though.

mmm......

"Sheep from Goats"

Separating such creatures one from the other sounds an easy job. Sheep are round and wooly and usually white with perhaps a bit of black, or if they disgrace their family black all over of course. Goats are hairy and angular. But it is not so easy to tell them apart on Halki as the little sheep are much more goaty....

and some goats can be a little sheepish no doubt?

Possibly

are
Anyway they all very Biblical looking and can clamber up the rocks and over the rough stone walls with marvellous speed and agility. Both are a true joy to behold and Halki is home to plenty of them, somwhere between 3012 and several billion.

HALKI IN MAY

Sunshine all the time (not at night of course) except during this most spectacular thunderstorm, a wonder to behold. We saw the great black clouds creeping upon us from the South West and anticipated some untimely showers but the first mighty flash and crash bang wallop caught us all unawares. But for the 'Grace of God' our Roger might well have spilled the first ouzo of the day.

absolutely unbeleeevable

It was a deluge; in through our window frames and under the doors, Soufoula's hens and brave cockerels all hid in mortal dread. We watched as the storm clouds went away across the sea, then saw them think better of it, regather and come all the way back to give us another blasting — wonderful.

phew.

Didn't it rain...

It's a pity most of that lovely water went to waste......

mmm...

page 59.

SPECIAL DELIVERY

Halkis' water has to come from Rhodes, delivered by a nice little ship, perhaps one day the island will get a desalination plant but meanwhile this is how the vital commodity is provided.

The water boat I was informed also supplies the famous island of Symi on the same round trip. This could explain why it arrived at our quayside horizontal and left sometime later having delivered our share sloping seriously uphill. From this we may deduce that our water was in the front and Symi's at the back, first class up front of course as in our theatres and aeroplanes. GOOD

BEFORE

AFTER

So what does Lugubrios mean?

DON'T ASK ME

Lugubrious (loo-goobri-əss, 1ə, 1oo-, 1ew-) adj. Mournful or Doleful, to an excessive degree. [Latin lūgugbris* mournful, from lūgēre to mourn].

* WRONG.

PAGE 60.

In our marvellously simple little kitchen, on the top of the fridge with a few other items are two earthenware pots, one marked COFFEE but containing sugar and the other marked SUGAR and containing coffee. No great surprise then that the hot tap delivered cold water and the cold occasionally hot, the drainage hole in the bathroom was distinctly uphill from the general level of the floor. Such observations simply increase ones respect for people who know how not to worry.

Soufoula has only one regulation for her visitors, THE BAG for the GOATS. Any rubbish that is edible, vaguely edible or very doubtful even must be put in a plastic bag for them and quite right too. It is probably the dietry supplements of tin cans plastic bottles and string that keep them so fit.

62

There certainly are donkeys on Halki but during our short visit for some reason they had all gone into hiding.

However no book about Greek islands would be complete without reference to donkeys so here it is.

They are creatures of modesty, beauty, humour and usefulness and as we all know the chosen form of transport of our Lord Jesus.

So thats alright then?

Absolutely

64

Dimitri, the handsome almost famously exuberant baker of Halki. His garrulous nature with the galloping antics and caperings along the quayside to greet ferryboats and to see off the departing ones is very much part of the 'Halki Experience,' and not to be missed.

there is a u' missing here.

An excellent baker he certainly is, to a certain extent we are told, this might be because he is married to hard working and patient Marina. They produce very good breads, cakes, buns, rolls, pizzas and various myserious Greek delicacies.

He's always cheery and smiling but especially this morning, for last night, while we were sleeping and he baking he became a grandfather.

GREEK PROVERB
FOR BAKERS

"You cannot have your caique and eat it."

ARCHIE PELAGO

lovely bread

Page No. 66.

unless of course your a barnacle...

HOME TERRITORY

Our kind hosts own three fine apartments ours being one of them, all part of their large house overlooking Emporio and its harbour. They also own land, rocky lumps of hillside where roam Soufoula's sheep and goats and nearer the house a random flock of chickens attended by several splendid cockerels.

A parcel of territory is rented by the Greek army and four or five young chaps inhabit a very pleasant little barracks up on the hill. Their task is simply to prevent an invasion by the Turks and they have a big gun of some sort, beneath a dusty tarpaulin to assist them. During our brief visit they were entirely successful and no Turkish invasions whatsoever took place.

good!

You can't blame the Greeks for being a bit edgy they've been invaded and occupied far more times than such lovely people deserve. Not just by the Turks of course but by Venetians, Italians, Germans, and indeed us too a long time ago when we were Crusaders and Knights of St. John, I just hope we were decently behaved when doing it.

Whatever the case we are certainly very warmly welcomed nowadays, dear Soufoula and Yiannis cannot stop giving us presents.

I'm really lovely

Lovely fish, dozens of eggs, bowls of shrimps, octopuses, lettuces, loaves, lemons, ouzo and the even more dangerous raki and all in copious quantities. As we said our farewells we recieved kisses, a rose each (even for us chaps) and several more giant lettuces 'for the journey.'

They enjoyed themselves didn't they?

Mmm... and made a lot of noise doing so.

Avzio.

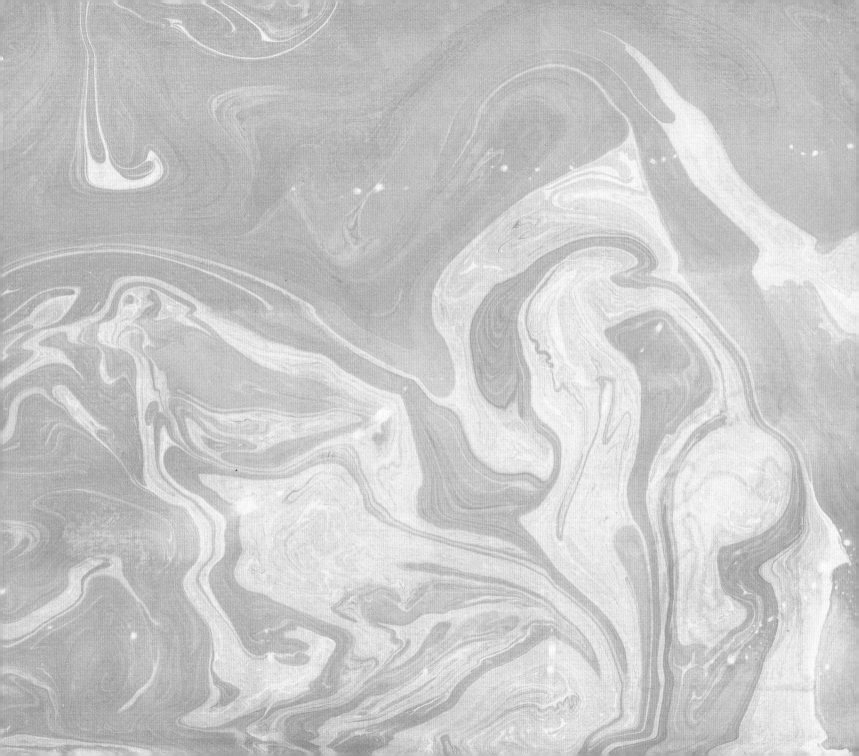